How to use the *Finally Fearless Workbook*:

This book is the companion workbook to use with
Finally Fearless: Journey from Panic to Peace

As you go through the main book, you will find lots of questions, exercises, and soul-searching activities that you'll find duplicated in here, with room to fill in your answers, plus additional questions to journal and reflect on.

Consider reading a chapter in that book first, then concurrently work on your assignments here. Each chapter in this workbook coincides with the same chapters in the main book. Take as much time as you need, as healing is a process. There is no hurry. Allow this workbook to function like a confidante, a friend to help you work out your thoughts.

Workbook Content:

Reflections – Bonus journal entries not included in the main book
Creations – Creative writings, poems
Quotations – Encouraging or inspiring quotes or Bible verses
Questions – Questions for the reader to answer or reflect on, journal assignments

Photos – Collections of original, black and white, peaceful photos to meditate on during anxious times. All original photography for the *Finally Fearless Workbook* was taken by photographer Christopher Price (©Christopher Price Pix, christopherpricepix.wordpress.com)

Finally Fearless Workbook

Journey from Panic to Peace

By Cheryl McKay

With original photography by Christopher Price

Purple PenWorks

By Cheryl McKay

Finally Fearless: Journey from Panic to Peace
Finally the Bride: Finding Hope While Waiting
Never the Bride (screenplay)
Never the Bride a novel (with Rene Gutteridge)
The Ultimate Gift (screenplay)
The Ultimate Life (co-writer / screenplay)
A Friend for Maddie (screenplay)
Gigi: God's Little Princess DVD (screenplay)
Wild & Wacky, Totally True Bible Stories Series (with Frank Peretti)

Coming Soon

Greetings from the Flipside a novel (with Rene Gutteridge)
Song of Springhill: a love story

For those who are
tired of fear
making their world smaller

FINALLY FEARLESS: JOURNEY FROM PANIC TO PEACE

Cover image by Lisa Crates Photography / lisacrates.us
Cover design by Christopher Price
All additional photography by Christopher Price
Purple PenWorks and feather artwork by Heather Gebbia

Published in the United States of America
Copyright © 2013 by Cheryl McKay
2013 — First Edition

TABLE OF CONTENTS

PART III: THE PEACE

PART I
The Panic

CHAPTER 1

Unmapped Territory:
The Moment Of Panic

When Jesus spoke again to the people, he said, "I am
the light of the world. Whoever follows me will never
walk in darkness, but will have the light of life."
(John 8:12)

This is your journey. I pray by the time you get through this workbook
and its accompanying book, *Finally Fearless: Journey from Panic to Peace*,
you will be a changed and healed person. I pray this time will be
enlightening, that God will show you what you need to work on and
how you can allow Him to help you heal.

It will be work. Trust me: that work will be worth it.

I think the best place for you to embark on this journey is through
prayer.

Ecclesiastes 11:10 says, "So then, banish anxiety from your heart and
cast off the troubles of your body."

PRAYER:

Write out a prayer of what you hope to get out of this study on fear and anxiety. Cite your goals. Invite God to join you in this journey:

_____

_____

_____

_____

_____

_____

_____

QUESTIONS:

Has your world shrunk? Have you found yourself avoiding situations that bring on an attack? Have you given up something you want because of the way your body and mind panic over it?

What scares you?
(Examples: driving on the freeway, waiting in lines, sitting tucked away in a booth at a restaurant, dating, social situations, public speaking)

A Look Inside (1987)

If anyone saw what was really inside, they'd reject me.
They'd close the door.
They'd slam it in my face.
If I can pretend to be more like them, I can fit in.
I can feel normal.
I can make it.
I can survive this tainted world.
Only if I can pretend.
Am I strong enough?
I can do this.
But will I ever let anyone see the real me?
Will I ever give anyone a look inside?

Do not be anxious about anything, but in everything, by prayer and petition, with thanksgiving, present your requests to God. And the peace of God, which transcends all understanding, will guard your hearts and your minds in Christ Jesus."

— Philippians 4:6-7

LIST YOUR ANXIETY SYMPTOMS:

Right before a full-blown attack:

During a full-blown attack:

A journal entry describing panic: "Throat closes, room spins. Stomach turns. Palms sweat. Breathing increases in pace. Yeah, with absurd acceleration. It all climaxes with the purging of my innards. No, this is not the flu or the result of some sickness. Not even the result of too much alcohol. It's the darkest moment no one can understand until they've gone through it themselves."

In God There's Hope (1986)

When I feel my heart is troubled,
And things won't ever be the same,
I try to look toward the future,
And think of life as just a game.
Even when my problems hurt,
And seem dragged out for long,
I need to remember the good times,
Always remember to move on.
Even though it's wishful thinking,
To always be problem-free,
We need to go back and pray to God,
That's the best solution for me.
The world is not a perfect place,
With problems we need to cope.
But remember we can look to God,
In Him there's always hope.

Cheryl's Journal (May 1986)

What is wrong with me? I get sick every time I see Kirk. I don't get it. It's so embarrassing. I hope he never finds out. I don't know anyone else who has this problem. I'm really weird. God, why can't I be normal like everyone else?

"*The only thing we have to fear is fear itself.*"
—Franklin D. Roosevelt

CHAPTER 2

Rough Terrain:
Anxiety Disorders

The worst fear is the fear of living.
(Theodore Roosevelt)

As I shared in the main book, I didn't know I had an anxiety disorder until many years after my first panic attack.

When did you first realize you had a problem with fear? Do you believe you have a panic disorder? Have you had panic attacks? Or are you just working through issues related to having fear in your life without having full-blown attacks?

What are you avoiding? What causes you to panic or feel fearful? List every person, place, or thing that triggers fear in you.

_____

_____

_____

_____

_____

_____

_____

How would you define anxiety? What words come to mind when you think of panic?

Webster's defines panic as "a sudden, unreasoning, hysterical fear, often spreading quickly." Anxiety is "a state of being uneasy, apprehensive, or worried about what may happen... an abnormal state like this, characterized by a feeling of being powerless and unable to cope with threatening events, typically imaginary, and by physical tension, as shown by sweating, trembling." (1) What do the words "typically imaginary" stir up in you?

In the main book, I cite many biblical examples of people who feared. Read one of those stories and journal about what you related to in that particular character's story? (Choose Adam & Eve, Abraham & Sarah, Moses, Gideon, David, or Elijah)

_____

_____

_____

_____

_____

_____

Anxiety tends to develop as a defense mechanism, whether we truly need protection from what we fear or not. Write a list of all possible events, people, circumstances, emotions, and objects that anxiety may be trying to protect you from. Brainstorm everything you can think of that you may consider to be a physical or emotional danger to you, whether it is actually dangerous or not. (Examples from my list include: to keep from getting hurt, rejected, abandoned, and protection from being too intimate with someone or opening my heart.)

Cheryl's Journal (June 1996)

Twice this week, I went to restaurants without even a thought about panic. Yay! The only time I remembered them is when I was halfway through the meal. But it was okay! No nervous problems. Finally, a victory! It's been a while since I've been able to eat comfortably in a restaurant. It's weird, considering I was never afraid of restaurants themselves. But just the fact that I had attacks in them before made me afraid. I hate how my world can get smaller and smaller because of where I had an attack. Thank God I can finally eat out again!

The Maze – a poem (2003)

I am caught in a maze,
One that dumps me on trails that lead to closed
doors,
Turned away faces,
There's a sorrow from a cry that never stops.
A place of solitude,
Of dying dreams,
Of a life not lived as one had hoped.

CHAPTER 3
Stormy Waters: Do We Sail Alone?

We also glory in our sufferings, because we know
that suffering produces perseverance; perseverance,
character; and character, hope. And hope does not put
us to shame, because God's love has been poured out
into our hearts through the Holy Spirit, who has been
given to us.
(Romans 5:3–5)

First and foremost, I want you to know you are not alone on your journey. As one of the most common emotional challenges that people face, we tend to have a lot in common with each other.

Of the following, highlight the traits you feel describe you:
Intelligent
Creative
Perfectionist
Insecure with low self-esteem
Control freak
Depressed

A quick Internet search will yield a list of famous people who've struggled with anxiety or panic disorders. Do a search and write down some names of those you recognize. Do any of those names surprise you? Do you find it comforting to know that even those who seem to have a lot going for them still have common struggles?

_____

_____

_____

_____

_____

_____

Choose one of those famous people who interests you. Do a little more research on that person. Try to find interviews where the person talks about their problem. Write down a list of things you relate to.

Do you feel you need to be perfect? If so, whose opinion matters to you most? Who is it you feel you need to be perfect for? Is this coming from you or them?

Do you feel like you need to be in control? If so, how does that show up in your life? Do you only need to be in control of some things or everything? What makes you feel out of control?

"Trust in the Lord with all thine heart and lean not unto thine own understanding; in all thy ways acknowledge him, and he shall direct thy paths." Proverbs 3:5–6 (kjv)

Since we seem to share common fears, take a look at the list below. Highlight the ones that apply to you:

Fear of abandonment

Fear of rejection

Fear of opinions of others

Fear of pain (physical or emotional)

Fear of risk

Fear of loss

Fear of death

Cheryl's Journal (December 23, 2001)

I look back on my teen life and wonder why I was so unhappy. I know my anxiety disorder certainly didn't help me. I always felt so abnormal. I never fit in. Very insecure. Never felt liked, accepted.

Write down what your dreams are for your life. What would you like to accomplish? Are your fears stopping you? If so, which fears? Has your anxiety disorder gotten in the way?

Make a list of goals you would try to reach if you had no fears about the consequences of trying. Make a list of what you feel you have to lose or gain.

Cheryl's Journal (June 1994)

I've been alone most of my life. Without a boyfriend. Yikes! Doesn't that sound like a pity party? Sometimes, I think emotionally, I am not normal or that I set myself up to get hurt, like I make it much harder on myself with my mind and imagination. Man, the things that run through my mind! There must be a reason, Lord, that You want me alone. Are You shaping me for something? Me and my fleshly self are sick of it. But I guess You know best.

"Courage is resistance to fear, mastery of fear, not absence of fear."

—Mark Twain

CHAPTER 4
Valleys:
When God Doesn't Heal...
Right Away

The wise man in the storm prays to God, not for safety
from danger, but for deliverance from fear.
(Ralph Waldo Emerson)

Have you ever wondered why God lets us suffer? Journal your feelings
about this question:

_____

_____

_____

_____

_____

Meditate upon the following verses:

Philippians 3:10-12 "I want to know Christ—yes, to know the power of his resurrection and participation in his sufferings, becoming like him in his death, and so, somehow, attaining to the resurrection from the dead. Not that I have already obtained all this, or have already arrived at my goal, but I press on to take hold of that for which Christ Jesus took hold of me."

What does it mean to participate in Christ's sufferings? Does this apply to suffering with panic, anxiety, or fear?

Do you feel like Jesus understands your suffering? If so, in which ways?

When Jesus asked His Father, "if you are willing, take this cup from me," do you think He was experiencing fear? (See Luke 22:42)

Take a look at John 16:33 "I have told you these things, so that in me you may have peace. In this world you will have trouble. But take heart! I have overcome the world." Jesus warned of troubles to come, but also encouraged us that these troubles are temporary. Are you encouraged to know your suffering will not last forever?

Why do you think God doesn't always heal us right away when we ask?

_____

_____

_____

_____

_____

_____

_____

The Bible clearly states, "For God hath not given us the spirit of fear; but of power, and of love, and of a sound mind" (2 Timothy 1:7 kjv). Fear does not come from God. Reflect on the following question: What would your actions be if you were released from your panic disorder? Is it possible the release from fear would lead you down a path toward sin?

_____

_____

_____

_____

_____

_____

Cheryl's Note to a Friend (March 19, 1996)

"Today, I heard a pastor preach that anxiety is a sin. That makes me beyond mad. I know we aren't supposed to be anxious about anything, yet I am not choosing to do this so-called sin in the same way we can choose whether to do the right or wrong thing. So in that sense, I disagree, and I don't think I am at fault for this. If I could control it, I would! And I'm doing everything to get better that I can possibly think of! What else is there to do? The pastor made a statement that you are not in prayer if you are anxious about anything and that is just plain ridiculous. I'm sure for some it's true, yes, but I have been in prayer. Tons! Especially about that issue."

Go back over your life and reflect on times when God has been faithful. There's no way to remember them all, but jot down what you do remember in a list, a list you can access whenever you feel you are losing faith. Write down times He's helped you get through something, supplied something you needed, or even just gave you a gift you wanted. The list can grow over time. Keep a record and add to it often.

Did God promise us that our lives would be perfect when we chose to follow Him? No. Actually, He tried to prepare us that sometimes, it would feel like the opposite. He promised trials, problems, and hard times, but He also promised never to leave us or forsake us (Hebrews 13:5). (Reflect on that verse.)

Are you angry with God for your trials?

I'd rather be angry than indifferent. Express my discontentedness, rather than stay silent. I sometimes feel so wronged. I'm just pouring out honesty here, Lord, not what's right to feel. I am so angry that I was robbed of a normal date life. I'm angry I've spent so many years alone. And now that I've dealt with issues that have kept me alone, why am I still alone? I have a huge void, yet I'm thirty years old. I'm angry about this, and I don't know how not to be. I wish my attitude could change so that I could praise You anyway, even when things don't turn out like I hope.

Psalm 34:14 (kjv) says, "Depart from evil, and do good; seek peace, and pursue it." What does it mean to pursue peace?

As you continue down this road, you are going to want God as your counselor. Write out a prayer asking for God to become your Wonderful Counselor.

Cheryl's Journal (April 16, 2002)

My life is so shallow. I work. I write. I daydream about the life I wish I had, the life I've been deprived of, that I wish for, cry for. I have these insatiable needs and wants. Please, dear God, change this!

"God, my efforts to make myself happy have yielded much unhappiness. My anxiety about my tomorrows steals the pleasure from my todays. And my anger toward my neighbor strangles my heart. Please release me from my preoccupation with myself and my troubles and begin filling me with Your indescribable joy. Amen."

— Prayer of St. Francis

PART II
The Journey

CHAPTER 5
Reading the Signs:
Guided Through Therapy

This chapter is where the real work begins. From the main book, this is the chapter full of the many questions I had to answer in therapy that helped me begin to understand why I had the problem I had and where it came from. Expect this section to take a while.

Answer as many of the questions in this chapter as possible. Skip the ones that don't apply to your situation. Take your time.

ANXIETY QUESTIONS:

In what situations can you predict that anxiety will happen?

Describe situations when you have experienced full-blown anxiety attacks.

Does panic keep you away from anything? Stop you from experiencing anything?

Is there a sinful side of anxiety? Consider what the Bible says about being anxious. Do you feel guilty for having anxiety? Is it a sign of a lack of faith? Is it a sin? (Reflect on Philippians 4:6)

Is there anything you are doing that is feeding this problem?

If fighting an attack makes it worse, what can you replace fighting with? What can you do instead? What will make you feel like you're being productive during an attack to stop it, without making it worse?

Do you need to know why you have an anxiety disorder? If so, why is it important that you pinpoint the cause?

What causes you to feel anxiety? (Ex. insecurity, fear of rejection)

How do you talk to and relate to people? How do you handle yourself socially?

Cheryl's Journal (May 1990)

I've always been afraid of guys and never trusted them. I can never let myself care about anyone. I have insecurities, which is strange because I'm not really an insecure person. Maybe it's easier if I just stay out of relationships, push people away.

And he will be called Wonderful Counselor, Mighty God, Everlasting Father, Prince of Peace.

— Isaiah 9:6b

Are there any friends who make you feel more comfortable during an anxiety attack? If so, describe what they do to help the situation. Pinpoint qualities in them that make you feel calmer. When they are around, do they bring out different qualities in you? Do you lose inhibitions?

Given your particular situation, describe how you'd be in that situation if you didn't panic. What would change?

What feelings does panic bring out of you?

What purpose does panic serve?

Personify your fear: What does it look like to you? Describe it as though it were a person in your life.

REJECTION QUESTIONS:

When in your life have you felt rejected? Did you know at the time it was a rejection? Was it really a rejection?

How do you deal with rejection? What mechanisms do you have to handle rejection?

What's the worst that can happen to you when you're rejected?

Evaluate exactly what is rejected: You as a person? A personality trait? An idea or belief that you hold? Is it likely the rejection has nothing to do with you personally? If it is you, does that mean something has to change? Are these changes for your own good? Or, if changes occur, are they only to please the person who did the rejecting?

What makes you feel intimidated by a person?

Cheryl's Journal (March 19, 1996)

I guess I have some tangible things I can try if I get into a dating situation again. I can see if any of these techniques work or help. But I don't understand why this is happening. I'm not sure if I need to know why in order to deal with it. My counselor says that just because I know some event caused me to feel fear doesn't mean my reactions to those situations will suddenly change. Knowing why doesn't fix the problem, but it is definitely part of the healing.

EMBARRASSMENT QUESTIONS:

When have you been humiliated?

What embarrasses you?

When have you been embarrassed because of your emotions? Were you just embarrassed to show them or were you embarrassed to feel them?

When have you hidden your emotions so you wouldn't be embarrassed?

Why do you hide truths about your life, like disappointments?

Do you fight tears when you need to cry? Do you only let yourself cry if you feel other people will think the situation warrants that reaction?

Are there situations where anyone reacted poorly to your emotions? Your tears? Has anyone ever told you that you shouldn't feel the way you're feeling, and therefore, invalidated your feelings?

UPBRINGING / FAMILY LIFE QUESTIONS:

Take a closer look at why you hide your troubles from friends or family. Do you have any past examples when you told them something that was hard to tell?

What would happen if you shared something that was bothering you emotionally?

What would happen if you shared an imperfection? A fault?

What role did image and appearances play in your upbringing?

MISCELLANEOUS QUESTIONS:

Do people's opinions of you affect what you think of yourself and your abilities (professionally and personally)?

In what areas are you afraid of taking risks?

How do you handle conflicts? Confrontations? Do you speak up when someone makes you angry? Can you clearly speak about your feelings?

How do you feel about change and uncertainty?

How do you handle loss? The fear of loss?

What does fear look like?

January 2003

The circle of a mind's life lives such a different cycle than reality's trails.

The blanks we fill in with pieces of our world, the pieces we wish would fit together in an order that would bring us the contentment and happiness we've been hoping for.

Longing for.

Praying for.

All the reflecting on a day's meaning does not bring to fruition the state we set our hopes in.

In the shadow of others, we walk alone, in silence.

Why do you always have to be in control?

Why do you feel like you are not worth the effort for people? Why do you feel unlovable?

Who accepts you unconditionally? What do they do to make you feel accepted? Is there anyone who does not accept you unconditionally?

When have you not gotten the attention you craved?

When have you not gotten the attention you needed?

What kinds of barriers do you have up? Why do you think they are there? What can you do to knock them down? Can you ask others to do anything to help you knock them down?

Write a list of all the benefits you have in your life because you have this problem.

Imagine you are a counselor. A woman who has your particular struggle comes into your office for help. What questions would you ask about her disorder? Her life? Her past? What areas do you feel would be important to discuss? Write down that list of questions. Consider answering them.

CHAPTER 6

Clearing Roadblocks: Travel Through the Past

In the main book, I share with you my very personal story of having to dig into my past to figure out what may have caused my anxiety disorder. I shared how through counseling, I was able to face the fact that the sexual abuse I endured as a child was that catalyst that brought a fear of men into my life.

Not everyone who has an anxiety disorder is going to have abuse as the cause, but many do.

In this part of your journal, I'd like to give you some space to do some of your own reflecting, to ponder whether anything from your past may be contributing to you having this problem in your life.

If you have no idea where your panic problem came from, go through old journals if you have any. Look for elements that can give you clues about what may have brought this on. They may also reveal previous times you experienced anxiety without realizing that's what was going on. If you ever wrote stories or poems, or if you gravitated toward particular types of books, movies, television shows, or songs, scour those for common themes.

Use the next couple pages to journal about anything you discover about yourself in reflecting on your past (whether you have old journals or not). Sometimes, understanding ourselves and where we've come from can help us get closer to healing. Where as I always felt like I was a freak for having this problem, once I finally admitted the abuse had something to do with it, I no longer felt so strange. I forgave myself for having my fears because I had uncovered a very real reason those fears showed up in the first place. Take the next couple pages to reflect on potential causes.

Is your anxiety disorder your way of protecting yourself from any abuse you've endured?

Have you been blaming God for your disorder, for allowing it to plague your life? Have you blamed another person?

(Short Story Excerpt from a story that should have told me I had problem with the abuse of my past:)

"The next thing she knew, he was undressing her. She cried out, but nothing mattered to him. He had no cares. And it happened. After a while, she got up with so much hate and anguish in her heart. She was beaten up on the inside. She felt cheap and worthless. She didn't know what to think or feel. She felt like crying. But it was like all of her emotions had been blocked off. She couldn't cry if she tried; but no one could soothe her pain."

Staying Young—A Poem (1986)

A confused little girl knows not what to do.
She wonders so much why life is so cruel.
Things run through her mind, like why she is now living.
And what her purpose is in life and why she is always giving.
Sometimes she feels so lonely, and she never gets anything back.
Like something important is missing which she feels
her life does lack.
Why should she go on living when problems are always here?
The hurt stays within her, and her heart feels like it's bare.
But she must face her problems and not give up and hide.
Even though it's like being shoved in a world with rules to abide.
Sometimes she wants the feelings of a child to stay within.
So she never has to grow up but stay young and always win.

If you discovered something from the past may be the cause, write down a list of people you'd like to talk to about your challenges who may be able shed light on your personal situation. But naturally, don't include anyone that put you in harm's way, especially in the case of an abuser. Seek outside counsel about any actions you may need to take.

Do you feel you need to forgive someone for your disorder? Did someone do something to you that you believe is the cause? Ask God to show you what you need to forgive.

Cheryl's Journal (April 1996)

I need someone to tell me it's okay to cry. I need someone to tell me that what happened to me was wrong. And what about later? Am I going to be able to get married? Will I ever be able to be intimate with a guy? I fear intimacy. Sexual expression is very emotional. So, if I fear showing emotions, how will I be able to do that? I fear my deepest longings.

CHAPTER 7
Cleansing Rain:
Healing Through Writing

"Courage is the price that life exacts for granting peace."
— Amelia Earhart

This is the creative chapter, where I ask you to take some time to play with these journal entries and writing assignments.

Write a scene that depicts your life. Write the role you wish you weren't playing, depicting your anxious self. Dramatize it. Exaggerate your story. Write a scene Julia Roberts would kill to play because she'd win another Oscar. Write the people in your lives the way you see them. Consider writing a scene leading up to an attack as well as a scene when an attack happens. Then, if you want to have a little fun with it, act out the scene in the privacy of your own room. (Feel free to type this exercise separately, so you have plenty of space.)

Is there a character you want to be? How about a person free from anxiety, a person doing and saying all the things you wish you could do or say? Write that scene. Create that character. Give the character a name you like. Put the character in situations where you've panicked in the past, only write the success. Write the version of the story you wish you could play in real life. Write a dialogue between that character and someone else. This can be a person in your life or a fictional person. Act this scene out privately; really get into the role. It may be awkward at first, but try to get into the scene. (You can use this experience later when you find yourself in the same situation in real life. Later, you can tap into how empowered you felt when you were acting out the anxiety-free version of the scene. Role-playing a scene where you don't have your usual panic attack can help build your confidence.) Write a synopsis of a scene you'll write:

Write a monologue from your point of view of the words you would use to tell someone for the first time about your anxiety struggles. You can write this like your personal story. It may help you in future situations when you have to tell someone for real. The more I told people my story, the more I got used to it. It can't hurt to practice at home.

Write a monologue you'd want for a dramatic theater audition. Really get into the angst of your story. Then, act it out. (This time, you're trying to win a Tony.)

Write the comic version in monologue style. Yes, you can find comedy when you learn to not take yourself so seriously. Write it as though you're a stand-up comic, making fun of yourself and your fears.

Write a short story of what it's like for you to go through a panic attack. Write in the first person. Use your inner monologue of what goes on inside your head. You will use this inner monologue in Chapter 10 when we rewrite the lies we tell our minds. This monologue can help you pinpoint that stream of junk that flies through your thoughts. Write this as though you're trying to make an outsider understand exactly how you feel—both emotionally and physically—during an attack. Give them a peek into what happens inside your mind.

The Holy Spirit & My Guardian Angel (1990)

Wherever I go, He follows. He's there.

Never do I walk alone.

He sees what's ahead.

He sees what I've left behind.

He taps my shoulder and daily does remind,

To walk in paths of goodness and mercy,

And to see, to open my eyes.

Conscience.

Awareness.

My reminder.

My Redeemer leaves me with One blessed by Him to intercede, to pray, to hold my hand, to try to lead.

He reminds me of the fundamental things I may have missed.

He's the image of God's Son, One who loves, respects, even if I'm not listening and am going to screw up.

God is the strength of my heart.

He never leaves me alone.

Besides His leading voice and pointing hand, He blesses me with a guardian angel to go with me throughout my day, in addition to His own leading strength, and His conscience, the Holy Spirit.

My Guardian hangs onto my car as I drive, keeps my foot from being snared, pushes away any imps that may try to push their way toward me in vain.

He stands guard over my bed at night while I sleep, never blinking or resting himself.

He's an extension of Jesus who sends workers and angels.

He releases with the command to protect.

I can walk and not fear.

For where I go, He goes.

When I cry, Jesus cries with me, holding my hand.

When I laugh, He laughs.

When I'm sick, He nurses me to health.

When I'm weak, He is my strength and holds up my head.

The Holy Spirit is my refining fire, my conscience.

God is my refuge and strength.

Jesus is my Savior, my life.

Writing poetry can be so healing. Don't feel like it has to rhyme. Write from your heart. Write the "whiny country song" version or the "angry rock" version.

Is there someone you feel doesn't understand you and you'd like the chance to say what you've been holding back? Is there someone you'd like to confront because of the way they've contributed to your disorder, like an abuser? Write the most honest letter you can. Say exactly what you always wished you could say but didn't have the guts. (This exercise is for you only. If later you decide you want to share that letter, make sure you seek outside counsel about it first.)

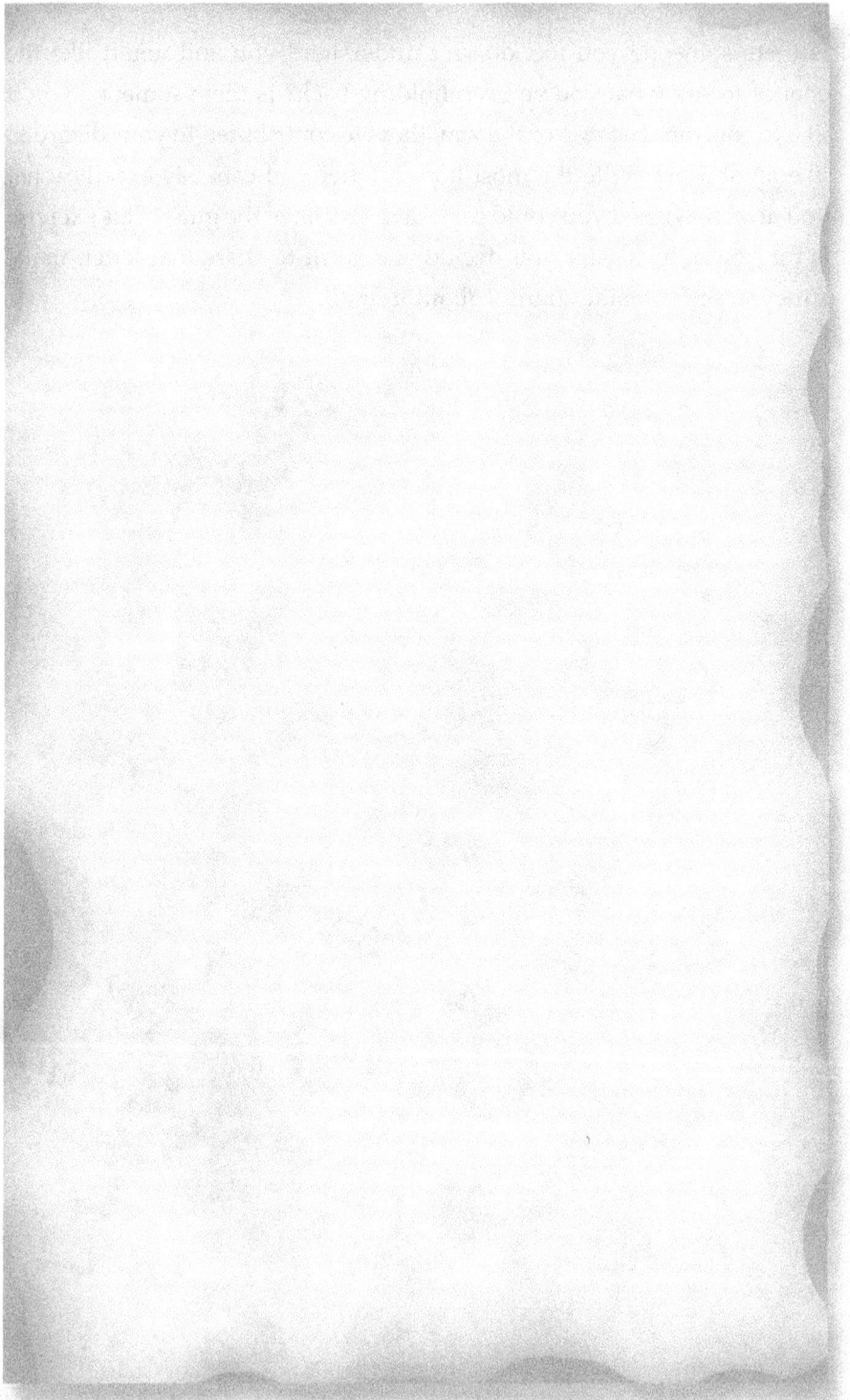

Write out a list of 10 things you really love about yourself. Try not to list accomplishments here. Try to list positive traits about you and your character—who you are that really defines what makes you unique, what makes you, *you*.

If you are unhappy with your life, what steps can you proactively take to change it? What steps will take you where you want to go? Make a list of goals and a list of proactive things you can do to improve your life or yourself. Start with small goals at first, then, graduate to bigger ones.

Something Missing is There – A Poem (1988)

You have to go through life,
With obstacles and mazes,
Adjusting to the world,
And all its crazy phases.
Your life had been so great,
Then things began to change,
Gradually you'd lose things,
Replaced by things so strange.
It can be hard to handle,
As much as you have to try,
Sorrow overcomes the joy,
But no one hears your cry.
Friends play a big part in your life,
But they don't always stick around,
You have to rely on yourself,
Not feeling so safe and sound.
How many times does life seem bad,
And that nothing is any good,
That no one's here to rely on,
You're always misunderstood.
Is suicide an answer?
You ask if it will work out.
Or is it just an escape,
From this world we know little about?
When faced with this alternative,
Things seem to grow so dim,
As though the door on the other side,
Will result in eternal sin.
What kind of escape is that,
To not try and work things through,
But to shut yourself right out,
And divide yourself in two.

Your life would be so great if it would,
Change back to the way it had been.
The smile doesn't return, you ask,
Will I ever be that happy again?
You don't know what to expect,
Or what the future holds.
But together we can work it out,
If we're confident and bold.
When you really love something,
You have to learn to let go.
If you try to hold on forever,
What you've missed, you'll never know.
Everyone's a small part of,
The world as one big whole.
But each work in different directions,
Not together to reach the goal.
When you feel scared or really hurt,
And you want it to go away.
There's an answer to what's missing,
Search, and you'll find the way.

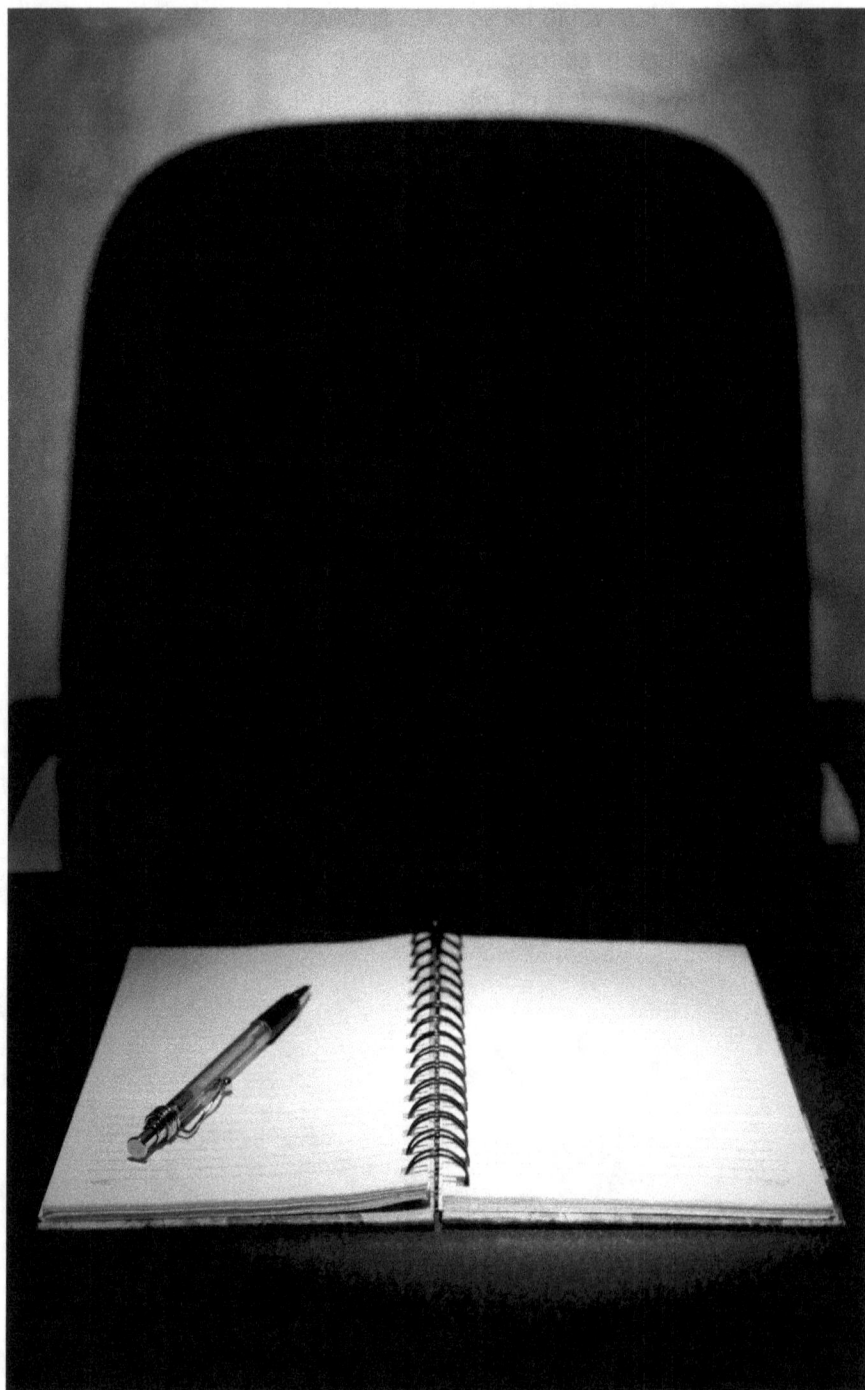

Think *Freaky Friday*. Consider someone's life you wish you had. What is it about that life you want? Would you take the bad along with it? The problems? Would it be worth it? What do you have in your life that this person probably wishes they had?

Make a list of ten things that scare you (people, places, events, situations). Then, make a list of ten things which bring you comfort. Are any of those ten comforts ones you can bring into situations that scare you? Can you bring a source of comfort into a source of anxiety? (For example, I mentioned in Chapter 1, when a trusted friend would show up during an attack, sometimes I was able to calm down.)

Write Psalm 151. Journal out your prayers to God. Try writing your prayers as though you are writing a Psalm that God could have published in the Bible. Psalms vary from complaints to prayers to poems of thanksgiving. I love the many examples in Scripture of regular people—like you and me—who poured out their pain to God in written form. Write honestly. Write lyrically, as though writing a song or poem.

CHAPTER 8

Travel Partners:
Telling Others

You gain strength, courage and confidence by every experience in
which you really stop to look fear in the face…
You must do the thing you cannot do.
(Eleanor Roosevelt)

It's time to get brave, venturing outside of this journal. It's time to choose someone to talk to about your challenges who you haven't told yet.

The first person outside my immediate family I told was my mother's sister, Jackie. I wrote her a letter. Choose one person you'd like to share your story with and draft a letter to them in this journal. Decide if you'd like to talk to them in person or by phone, or send a letter like the one you draft here. Writing your thoughts out first may help you decide what you'd like to share.

Make a list of friends or family members you haven't talked to about your problem yet. Then make a plan to tell them.

_____

_____

_____

Can you think of anyone in your life that you suspect may share your challenges with fear, panic, or anxiety? Write down their names. Decide if and when you'd like to reach out to them and share. (I found that in sharing with friends, I was so surprised by how many shared my history and similar challenges.)

_____

_____

_____

Do an internet search for message boards that discuss panic or anxiety disorders. Sign up for a screen-name. You can create an alias and stay anonymous if you'd like. Post your first note, to share a bit about yourself, and see what kind of support you get in return. Write your favorite website names or forum names here:

On those same message boards, read other people's stories. Does anyone sound like they're struggling in similar ways? Write down a list of those you'd like to post responses to, and see if you can become an encouragement to someone else.

Cheryl's Journal (June 18, 2001)

I had a great time this weekend hanging out with guys. I think it planted a seed in me to want a relationship. But when we were sitting by the pool and that girl said that Richard likes me, I got so nervous. Suddenly, I didn't feel "okay" anymore. I didn't get sick, but I didn't feel well either. And it's been over five years since therapy. This scares me a lot. Am I no better? When will this ever be over? This is definitely a problem that draws me to prayer, but I still hope for a healing.

Prepare an outline for a testimonial, the talk you'd be willing to share with a group sometime. (It took years before I was willing to do this, but sharing in groups has huge rewards. There is bound to be someone there who relates to you and thought he or she was alone!)

Make a list of any other ways you feel led to share. (Ex. Write a book. Lead a support group at your church or community center.)

Cheryl's Journal (September 9, 2001)

Progress... this is what I'm seeing in my life. Thank you, God. I don't know if I were dating someone else if I'd still be okay. But dating Richard has been so healthy for me. A very good chance to be vulnerable and tell about my problem, be up-front, while still feeling accepted for my problems.

Cheryl's Journal (January 11, 2002)

My life lately has gotten a lot more open. I've had to get used to talking about my past, both to my parents and my friends. It's been such a growth experience for me. I am making progress with this panic stuff, just by being open. It's nice to see my mother reach out and do what she can to help me. (Giving me books and tapes and doing her own research.) She never had that chance before. It's nice to see her take an active part in trying to help me.

PART III
The Peace

CHAPTER 9

Paving the Way:
Roads Toward Peace

I have learned this at least by my experiment: that if one
advances confidently in the direction of his dreams, and
endeavors to live the life which he has imagined, he will
meet with a success unexpected in common hours.
(Henry David Thoreau)

This chapter contains a lot of exercises and coping methods for those
times when you are experiencing anxiety and panic attacks. In the main
book, I discussed many coping methods. They are listed below. Highlight
ones you're interested in trying. (Please note: many of these need to be
practiced when you are not in the middle of an attack.)

Breathing Exercises	Therapy
Relaxation	Massage
Self-Talk/Positive Thinking	Scripture
Visualization	Aroma Therapy
Humor	Medication
Distractions	Reading
Prayer	Television/Movies
Exercise	Music
Meditation	Desensitization

If you have an anxiety attack, start by asking yourself the right questions during an attack:

What am I doing that could be contributing to this panic?

What can I do to help myself now?

List other coping methods you know of or have tried:

_____

_____

_____

_____

_____

_____

_____

Cheryl's Journal (July 2001)

*T*oday marked my first date in over five years. Wow. And I did it without anxiety attacks. I used pills two times today, and it really helped. I even ate! To make the situation safer for me, I suggested we eat much later in the day. That gave me about seven hours to not eat, to relax a bit, get used to him, then eat dinner. I think controlling the circumstances made a big difference. I felt in control. I took one pill right before the date and another shortly before dinner. And it worked! Wow! A successful date. I didn't know I had it in me.

The rest of this workbook chapter has exercises to help you cope with anxiety attacks:

Relaxation Exercises

TENSE / RELEASE EXERCISE:

Lie down on the floor. Tense your body for ten seconds then relax your body for the next ten. Try it several times. Then write below how your body feels during both states. Be descriptive. Did you notice if you held your breath while you were tense? Repeat the exercise again. This time, afterwards, get up and walk around. Do you feel calmer than before you started the exercise? This exercise is intended to get you used to focusing on your body during a time of tension and relaxation, so you can recognize both states. Did the moment you were tense start to make you feel anxious? If so, your body is associating those tensions with an anxiety attack.

BREATHING EXERCISE:

Lie on the floor. Practice breathing from your diaphragm. Take ten seconds to inhale, another ten to exhale. Pay attention to how your lower abdomen moves up and down. Concentrate on breathing deep, cleansing breaths. Do this ten times lying on your back on the floor, feeling your stomach's movements. Then, do it ten times while standing or walking around. This can help you get used to deep, cleansing breaths while active, a skill that is important during an attack.

Sometimes, breathing properly can slow symptoms down, even if they don't stop completely. If you do feel symptoms coming on, take a quick inventory of how you're breathing. Are you breathing too fast or too shallow?

If you do the exercise, you'll start to memorize how it feels to take deep breaths. You'll know right away if you're not breathing deeply enough. If you feel panic coming on, let your mind focus on breathing; it gives you something active to do. Breathing is an important ally during a panic attack. We have to get (or keep) control of it. It can help or hurt us, depending on how we use it. If you breathe too rapidly or shallowly, you'll make yourself even more anxious. You could bring on hyperventilation.

VISUALIZATION ASSIGNMENTS:

In the main book, I talked about the healing ability of pictures. To follow are assignments to help you put this into practice.

Take a situation that brings on anxiety. (For example, a trip in a car, an elevator, a date, a grocery store line, or sitting in a restaurant.) Imagine yourself facing that fear without having a panic attack. Watch yourself go through the motions without fear. Write down how this makes you feel. Write down what you did in your imagination; emotionally capture your success.

Come up with a list of at least five of your favorite Bible verses that encourage peace. Memorize them. Come up with a visual picture for the verse. You can bring this image to memory during an attack. It will help pull you into a right brain, heart function. It works better than only reciting the words of the verse.

Example:

Verse: Psalm 94:19: "When anxiety was great within me, your consolation brought me joy."

Picture: Imagine yourself on a peaceful hillside, sitting on the grass next to Jesus, His arm around you as you say these words to Him. Imagine His smile, His kind eyes.

"Create your safe place"

Create in your mind a place you feel is safe. This can be real or imaginary. It can be pieces of many different places you've been where you felt peaceful. There aren't any rules. Let it be a place you can retreat to – in your mind – when you're experiencing anxiety. Postcards from resort towns are a great source of God's beauty. You can paint your own picture in your mind. Or, if you're an artist, you may want to sketch or paint this place as well. You could use an actual photograph if you have one. (We have original, black and white photographs in this workbook that can be used. Look at the photos, close your eyes and imagine yourself in that peaceful setting. See several samples to follow.)

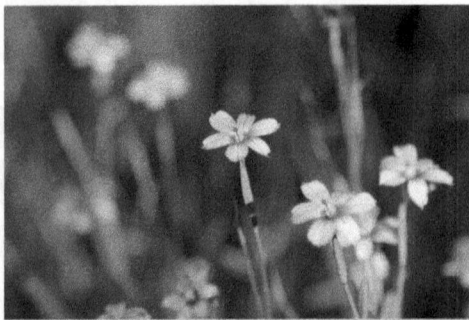

We discussed the concept of desensitization in the main book, a way to practice in baby steps exposing yourself to your fears. List steps you could take to practice. (Example, when I developed a fear for eating in restaurants after having so many panic attacks in them, I had to work my way up to it again. Starting with eating at a picnic in the park, then on patios, then at a table and not a booth where I would feel trapped. That was a good progression to get used to successfully eating in restaurants again.)

Cheryl's Journal (November 18, 2001)

It was our first date where I didn't take a pill. I was only nervous when I wasn't sure what was going to happen next in the evening. I felt slightly nauseated, and I wasn't breathing normally. So, I started feeling light-headed. But here are the positives: I didn't have an attack. I didn't overreact to the symptoms. I don't think any of my anxiousness showed. Thank you, Lord, that I'm near the end of this problem.

Make a list of goals you want to accomplish to battle your anxiety disorder: progress you'd like to make, actions you'd like to take without anxiety. Think of small steps first, then, set larger goals.

My Goals

Note Cards

Keep little note cards in your purse, book bag, or back pocket that remind you of your coping techniques when you're too frazzled to think straight. My cards ranged from breathing techniques to descriptions of visual pictures to peaceful Bible promises. (At the end of this book is a list of many Bible verses you can copy down onto cards relating to peace, trust, and handling fears.)

Make a list of the note cards you'd like to make:

Dreams/Visions

Daniel, in the Old Testament, says the reason you dream is so you can "know the thoughts of thy heart" (Daniel 2:30, kjv). Psalm 16:7 says, "I will praise the Lord, who counsels me; even at night my heart instructs me."

Have you had any dreams lately that you feel should be recorded, that may be helpful regarding your anxiety disorder? Has God shown you any pictures or visions? (If you start to get dreams or visions regularly, record them all in a notebook or journal.) If you have, write down one sample here and a list of symbols and potential interpretations.

Dream/Vision:

"Anxiety in human life is what squeaking and grinding are in machinery that is not oiled. In life, trust is the oil."

— Henry Ward Beecher

Interpretation:

Dream/Vision:

Interpretation:

CHAPTER 10
A New Map:
Rewriting the Lies

So do not fear, for I am with you; do not be dismayed, for I am your
God. I will strengthen you and help you; I will uphold you with my
righteous right hand.
-Isaiah 41:10

In the main book, I systematically rebuffed a lot of lies that I would tell
myself through either the truth of God's Word or through any fresh ideas
I felt like God gave me to deal with that particular lie. Now, it's your turn.
For this workbook chapter, I will give you space to combat the lies that
have been streaming through your mind. (If you wrote the short story
depicting what goes on inside your mind during an attack in Chapter 7,
feel free to use it now to compile these lies.)

Make a list of all the lies you tell yourself:

Right before a full-blown attack:

During a full-blown attack:

I'll repeat a few examples in this workbook of lies I refuted in the main chapter, so you can have a format to follow in working on your own lies.

The first two examples are refuting a lie with the Word of God:

LIE: **Everything I tell myself, in my mind, is truth**.

TRUTH: Many lies that stream through our minds are from the devil himself, who wants us to be defeated. He is the author of lies.

John 8:44b: "[The devil] was a murderer from the beginning, not holding to the truth, for there is no truth in him. When he lies, he speaks his native language, for he is a liar and the father of lies."

The devil is the one who brings on fear, not God.

LIE: **Anxiety lives in me, and I can't get rid of it.**

TRUTH: We may feel like anxiety lives in us because it takes over our whole body. But it doesn't need to stay there. If we've asked Him to, we have a Savior who has taken up residence in our hearts.

Galatians 2:20a (kjv): "I am crucified with Christ: nevertheless I live; yet not I, but Christ liveth in me."

2 Timothy 1:7 (kjv): "For God hath not given us the spirit of fear; but of power, and of love, and of a sound mind."

* * *

The second set of examples is refuting the lies with God's fresh revelation, relating to my specific situation or prayer lifted up to Him.

LIE: **I am different; no one else has this problem. Other people are normal. Why am I the only one this is happening to? No one else is this stupid.**

TRUTH: No one is perfect. Everyone has something they must deal with, something they wish weren't part of their lives. While it's true that not everyone has an anxiety disorder, we shouldn't feel insignificant or assume others are superior to us because they don't have this particular problem. Statistics show how extremely common this problem is!

When I prayed about these feelings, this is what I feel God said to me: "My daughter, do not speak poorly of yourself. Do not put yourself down. I am here to build you up. Every child of Mine is different. You are wonderfully made by My hand. You can find your restoration in Me."

LIE: **I am out of control; I'm a failure when I can't control it. I must be in control always. I am not allowed to get sick.**

TRUTH: I am created by God. Therefore, I am not a failure no matter what I do or what happens to me. I don't have to be in control of my anxiety at all times. I need to surrender to God my desire to be in control of everything. God has told me more than once that He is the one in control. I don't have to be. That's a relief!

Take the next set of pages of this workbook to work on refuting some of your lies. You can choose to refute them with God's Word or ask Him to speak to you directly about your situation, or a mix of both.

"What a man thinks of himself, that it is which determines, or rather indicates, his fate."

—Henry David Thoreau

LIE:

TRUTH:

LIE:

TRUTH:

LIE:

TRUTH:

Cheryl's Journal (August 4, 1996)

Wow! Great victory today. First encounter with Nathan with no anxiety, fretting, attacks, and sickness. Yet, last month I was in dire straights. Praise God. What a victory. Finally, some success. I took a pill as a cushion, but in my heart I knew I didn't need it. I was already calm when I took it. The big thing I learned here was that my victory wasn't based on any breathing or relaxation technique. I didn't get to a point where I needed those. Instead, I had victory with my thoughts and beliefs. They were the most important things to battle. I used some thought-stopping and just tried not to plan or think about the situation. That did a world of good because I didn't let myself imagine a catastrophe waiting to happen. Also, I believed I could do it. Since I believed in myself it gave me a new confidence I haven't had before. I'm surprised I was so confident since I've had zero success yet. That is, until now! But I had no physical symptoms telling me I'd fail. Then, I claimed victory. Thank God.

LIE:

TRUTH:

LIE:

TRUTH:

LIE:

TRUTH:

Cheryl's Note to a Friend (March 24, 1996)

"Some of it, I'm sure, is a learned pattern of responses that I need to reprogram. Sometimes, I can make it worse on myself by saying, 'Okay, I'm going on a date. Dates make me sick. Therefore, this date will make me sick.' I talk myself into it because I'm used to it."

Cheryl's Journal (1998)

I despise when people ask when I'm going to get married or involved like I'm "supposed to." Why do they get to define what's normal? It's so annoying. Maybe I am abnormal in this area. Maybe they're right.

LIE:

TRUTH:

LIE:

TRUTH:

LIE:

TRUTH:

"When anxiety was great within me, your consolation brought me joy."

— Psalm 94:19

LIE:

TRUTH:

LIE:

TRUTH:

LIE:

TRUTH:

LIE:

TRUTH:

LIE:

TRUTH:

LIE:

TRUTH:

In the main book, I discussed potential oppressions of the enemy and put a name on all that I wanted to pray against. I'll include my list here. Highlight any you relate to:

Fear, anxiety, panic, mistrust, fear of rejection, perfectionism, inadequacy, self-loathing, shame, suicide, death, hopelessness, loneliness, depression, despair, bitterness, unforgiveness, resentment, and anger.

Do you have any of your own to list? Pray them out in Jesus' name with the authority He's given to us. (This is a good kind of prayer to have someone else or a group pray with you.)

Luke 10:19, "I have given you authority to trample on snakes
and scorpions and to overcome all the power of the enemy;
nothing will harm you."

Cheryl's Journal (1997)

I'm trying to change some of these ways of thinking. My worth is in Christ alone, not my talent, abilities, possessions, or what others say and think about me. I need to also stop demanding I be perfect and stop saying mean things to myself.

CHAPTER 11

Yield to God:
Face Your Biggest Fear

*I believe that anyone can conquer fear by doing the
things he fears to do.*
(Eleanor Roosevelt)

Has God asked you to face your biggest fear yet? What do you imagine that would be?

_____

_____

_____

_____

_____

Do you need healing from something very specific, like I did (as shared in the main book) from being told I wasn't a treasure?

Do you feel like you are in some kind of a wilderness season? Do you want to get out? Are you complaining about God not letting you out? If so, it's time to invite Him in and let Him show you the way out. Journal your prayer now:

In the main book, I shared a story about how I had been angry with God for the pain He allowed as a result of me obeying Him. It wasn't until I was able to let go of my anger regarding that, that healing could come. I used the parallel in the question of whether or not Jesus would have wanted to curse God for all of the pain He experienced in following God's will. How does this illustration make you feel? Does it help you in dealing with any of the pain you may be experiencing due to no fault of your own? Due to obedience?

Cheryl's Journal (1986)

Oh Lord, I love You very much. I know I can always count on You and not any human beings. You're the only one who is there for me always. When I feel down or upset, I know Your precious arms are around me. Human hands are only around temporarily, but Your spiritual arms and love never leave me.

CHAPTER 12

The Destination: Still Waters

The Lord is my shepherd; I shall not want.
He maketh me to lie down in green pastures;
He leadeth me beside the still waters.
(Psalm 23:1–2, kjv)

What's does your "Still Waters" destination look like?

Journal any victories you have experienced since starting this study on fear and anxiety:

_____

_____

_____

_____

_____

_____

_____

_____

_____

"Live your beliefs and you can turn the world around."
— Henry David Thoreau

Reflect on the progress you've made so far:

Write out a final prayer in this workbook about where you hope to go from here in your journey toward peace:

I applaud you for going through this whole workbook. This is no easy task. But the work is well worth it, if it means finding peace and healing from your fears and anxieties. I encourage you to continue on this journey toward peace. Don't give up. Cling to God and allow Him to continue to be that Wonderful Counselor that He is.

Topical Bible Verses

<u>ANXIETY/WORRY</u>

(Psalm 94:19) When anxiety was great within me, your consolation brought me joy.

(Proverbs 12:25) Anxiety weighs down the heart, but a kind word cheers it up.

(Ecclesiastes 2:22) What do people get for all the toil and anxious striving with which they labor under the sun?

(Ecclesiastes 11:10a) So then, banish anxiety from your heart and cast off the troubles of your body…

(Matthew 6:25) Therefore I tell you, do not worry about your life, what you will eat or drink; or about your body, what you will wear. Is not life more important than food, and the body more important than clothes?

(Matthew 6:34a) Therefore do not worry about tomorrow, for tomorrow will worry about itself…

(Philippians 4:6-7) Do not be anxious about anything, but in everything, by prayer and petition, with thanksgiving, present your requests to God. And the peace of God, which transcends all understanding, will guard your hearts and your minds in Christ Jesus."

(1 Peter 5:7) Cast all your anxiety on him because he cares for you.

FEAR

(Psalm 23:4) Even though I walk through the darkest valley, I will fear no evil, for you are with me; your rod and your staff, they comfort me.

(Psalm 27:1) The LORD is my light and my salvation — whom shall I fear? The LORD is the stronghold of my life — of whom shall I be afraid?

(Psalm 27:3) Though an army besiege me, my heart will not fear; though war break out against me, even then will I be confident.

(Proverbs 1:33) But whoever listens to me will live in safety and be at ease, without fear of harm.

(Isaiah 41:10) So do not fear, for I am with you; do not be dismayed, for I am your God. I will strengthen you and help you; I will uphold you with my righteous right hand.

(Isaiah 41:13) For I am the LORD your God who takes hold of your right hand and says to you, Do not fear; I will help you.

(Isaiah 43:1b) …Do not fear, for I have redeemed you; I have summoned you by name; you are mine.

(Isaiah 54:4a) Do not be afraid; you will not be put to shame. Do not fear disgrace; you will not be humiliated…

(Isaiah 54:14b) …you will have nothing to fear. Terror will be far removed; it will not come near you.

(Jeremiah 39:17) But I will rescue you on that day, declares the LORD; you will not be given into the hands of those you fear.

(Haggai 2:5b) ...And my Spirit remains among you. Do not fear.

(2 Timothy 1:7, kjv) "For God hath not given us the spirit of fear; but of power, and of love, and of a sound mind."

(1 John 4:18) There is no fear in love. But perfect love drives out fear, because fear has to do with punishment. The one who fears is not made perfect in love.

TRUST

(Psalm 9:10) Those who know your name trust in you, for you, LORD, have never forsaken those who seek you.

(Psalm 20:7) Some trust in chariots and some in horses, but we trust in the name of the LORD our God.

(Psalm 22:4) In you our ancestors put their trust; they trusted and you delivered them.

(Psalm 25:2) I trust in you; do not let me be put to shame, nor let my enemies triumph over me.

(Psalm 31:14) But I trust in you, LORD; I say, "You are my God."

(Psalm 33:21) In him our hearts rejoice, for we trust in his holy name.

(Psalm 37:3) Trust in the LORD and do good; dwell in the land and enjoy safe pasture.

(Psalm 37:5a) Commit your way to the LORD; trust in him...

(Psalm 52:8b) I trust in God's unfailing love forever and ever.

(Psalm 56:3) When I am afraid, I put my trust in you.
(Psalm 56:11) In God I trust and am not afraid. What can man do to me?

(Psalm 62:8) Trust in him at all times, you people; pour out your hearts to him, for God is our refuge.

(Psalm 91:2) I will say of the LORD, "He is my refuge and my fortress, my God, in whom I trust."

(Psalm 115:11) You who fear him, trust in the LORD—he is their help and shield.

(Psalm 143:8) Let the morning bring me word of your unfailing love, for I have put my trust in you. Show me the way I should go, for to you I entrust my life.

(Proverbs 3:5–6) Trust in the LORD with all your heart and lean not on your own understanding; in all your ways submit to him, and he will make your paths straight.

(Proverbs 29:25) Fear of man will prove to be a snare, but whoever trusts in the LORD is kept safe.

(Isaiah 12:2) Surely God is my salvation; I will trust and not be afraid. The LORD, the LORD himself is my strength and my defense; he has become my salvation.

(Isaiah 26:4) Trust in the LORD forever, for the LORD, the LORD himself, is the Rock eternal.

(Jeremiah 39:18) "I will save you; you will not fall by the sword but will escape with your life, because you trust in me," declares the LORD.

(Nahum 1:7) The LORD is good, a refuge in times of trouble. He cares for those who trust in him.

FAITHFUL

(2 Chronicles 20:20b) Have faith in the LORD your God and you will be upheld.

(Psalm 33:4) For the word of the LORD is right and true; he is faithful in all he does.

(Psalm 145:13b) …The LORD is trustworthy in all his promises and faithful in all he does.

(1 Corinthians 1:9) God is faithful, who has called you into fellowship with his Son, Jesus Christ our Lord.

(1 Thessalonians 5:24a) The one who calls you is faithful…

(2 Thessalonians 3:3) But the Lord is faithful, and he will strengthen you and protect you from the evil one.

(Hebrews 10:23) Let us hold unswervingly to the hope we profess, for he who promised is faithful.

ENCOURAGEMENT/HOPE

(Psalm 10:17) You, LORD, hear the desire of the afflicted; you encourage them, and you listen to their cry.

(Romans 15:4) For everything that was written in the past was written to teach us, so that through endurance taught in the scriptures and the encouragement they provide we might have hope.

(2 Thessalonians 2:16-17) May our Lord Jesus Christ himself and God our Father, who loved us and by his grace gave us eternal encouragement and good hope, encourage your hearts and strengthen you in every good deed and word.

(Hebrews 6:18) God did this so that, by two unchangeable things in which it is impossible for God to lie, we who have fled to take hold of the hope set before us may be greatly encouraged.

PEACE

(Numbers 6:26) The LORD turn his face toward you and give you peace.

(Judges 6:23) But the LORD said to him, "Peace! Do not be afraid. You are not going to die."

(Psalm 29:11) The LORD gives strength to his people; the LORD blesses his people with peace.

(Psalm 34:14) Turn from evil and do good; seek peace and pursue it.

(Psalm 85:8a) I will listen to what God the LORD says; he promises peace to his people, his faithful servants…

(Isaiah 9:6b) …And he will be called Wonderful Counselor, Mighty God, Everlasting Father, Prince of Peace.

(Isaiah 26:3) You will keep in perfect peace those whose minds are steadfast, because they trust in you.

(Isaiah 26:12) LORD, you establish peace for us; all that we have accomplished you have done for us.

(Isaiah 32:17) The fruit of that righteousness will be peace; its effect will be quietness and confidence forever.

(Jeremiah 33:6) Nevertheless, I will bring health and healing to it; I will heal my people and will let them enjoy abundant peace and security.

(John 14:27) Peace I leave with you; my peace I give you. I do not give to you as the world gives. Do not let your hearts be troubled and do not be afraid.

(John 16:33) I have told you these things, so that in me you may have peace. In this world you will have trouble. But take heart! I have overcome the world.

(Romans 15:13) May the God of hope fill you with all joy and peace as you trust in him, so that you may overflow with hope by the power of the Holy Spirit.

(1 Corinthians 14:33a) For God is not a God of disorder but of peace...

(Philippians 4:7) And the peace of God, which transcends all understanding, will guard your hearts and your minds in Christ Jesus.

(Colossians 3:15) Let the peace of Christ rule in your hearts, since as members of one body you were called to peace. And be thankful.

(1 Thessalonians 5:23) May God himself, the God of peace, sanctify you through and through. May your whole spirit, soul and body be kept blameless at the coming of our Lord Jesus Christ.

(2 Thessalonians 3:16) Now may the Lord of peace himself give you peace at all times and in every way. The Lord be with all of you.

CHAPTER NOTES

Chapter 2

1. Agnes, Michael, Editor in Chief. *Webster's New World College Dictionary*. (CA: IDG Books Worldwide, Inc., 2000, 4th edition). p. 64, 1040.

ABOUT THE AUTHOR

Cheryl McKay has been professionally writing since 1997. Cheryl wrote the screenplay for *The Ultimate Gift*, based on Jim Stovall's novel. The award-winning film stars James Garner, Brian Dennehy, and Abigail Breslin and was released in theaters by Fox in 2007. *The Ultimate Gift* won a Crystal Heart Award at the Heartland Film Festival, received three Movieguide Nominations, winning one of the Ten Best Family Films of 2007, and won a CAMIE Award, for one of the Top Ten Films of the year. Cheryl also wrote the DVD for *Gigi: God's Little Princess*, another book adaptation based on the book by Sheila Walsh, as well as the *Wild and Wacky, Totally True Bible Stories* audio series and books with Frank Peretti. She wrote a half hour drama for teenagers about high school violence, called *Taylor's Wall*. It was produced in Los Angeles by Family Theater Productions. McKay wrote a script called *Greetings from the Flipside*, commissioned by Art Within, after winning a year-long fellowship. It's being novelized for B&H Publishing with Rene Gutteridge. Her screenplay, *Never the Bride*, has been adapted into a novel for Random House Publishers and was released in June 2009. It won Best Women's Fiction book at the Carol Awards/Book of the Year Awards at ACFW and was a finalist in the top three Women's Fiction books at the Inspirational Reader's Choice Awards. She also co-wrote *The Ultimate Life* for ReelWorks. And she released *Finally the Bride: Finding Hope While Waiting*, a book for singles losing hope while waiting to find love.

(Photo Credit: Vincent Wallace / Silver Hill Images)

Visit Cheryl's Website at:

www.purplepenworks.com

Visit Cheryl's Blog at:

cherylmckay.wordpress.com

Visit Cheryl's Twitter: @PurplePenWorks

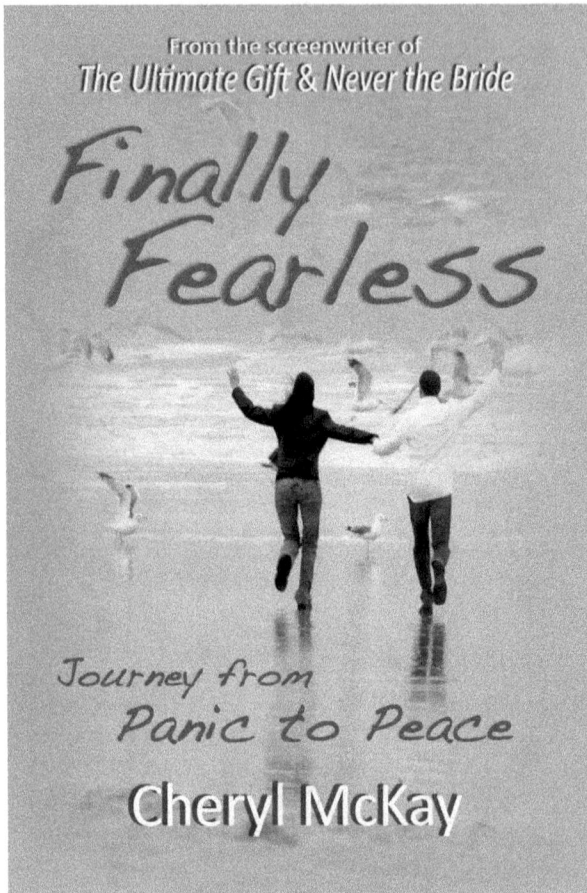

From the screenwriter of
The Ultimate Gift & Never the Bride

Finally Fearless

Journey from Panic to Peace

Cheryl McKay

"This is one courageous book. In her bravest turn yet, Cheryl McKay dives into the storm-tossed depths of suffocating anxiety. It is a work of faith in its most practical and sometimes harrowing expression. This unflinchingly honest, soul-baring account is the personal hand of experience, reaching out across the churning seas of fear, guiding all who would read to still waters and lasting peace."

— **Susan Rohrer**, author of THE HOLY SPIRIT: Amazing Power for Everyday People & IS GOD SAYING HE'S THE ONE?: Hearing from Heaven about That Man in Your Life

From Cheryl's Journal:
Why am I like this? What is wrong with me? Why am I so afraid? I can't
control my anxiety; these fears seem to overtake me. Does anyone know how I
feel? No one else has this problem. I am a freak, and I am alone. Where is God
in this?

Do fear and anxiety rule your life?

They used to rule mine. This is the book I was too afraid to write and definitely too afraid to publish. That would mean others could read some of my most private thoughts, pieces of my most difficult and painful journey. Most of my life, I put on a good face, that "life is perfect" façade. It was a sham. Then I realized I had to face my problems, my past, and my fears if I ever wanted to live a normal, healthy life. In writing this book, I decided to join the imperfect human race. I wrote it because I needed to heal. Maybe you need to heal, too.

Through writing about my story of panic, fear, and seemingly irrational anxieties, I uncovered so much about panic and anxiety disorders, coping techniques, causes of anxiety and fear, soul-searching activities to help unearth the root of anxiety problems, and methods that can bring about healing. After many years of stagnancy, I found hope. God walked me through every step to help me find ways to grow, heal, change, and climb out from under the relentless thumb of anxiety. I can honestly say I am now healed.

Are you tired of fighting against your fears? Has panic interrupted your life? Has anxiety stopped you from going after your dreams? I encourage you to read my story and start your soul-searching journey now so you, too, can venture toward peace.

Finally Fearless: Journey from Panic to Peace is filled with practical advice, exercises, personal stories, and tangible ways for readers to participate in their healing.

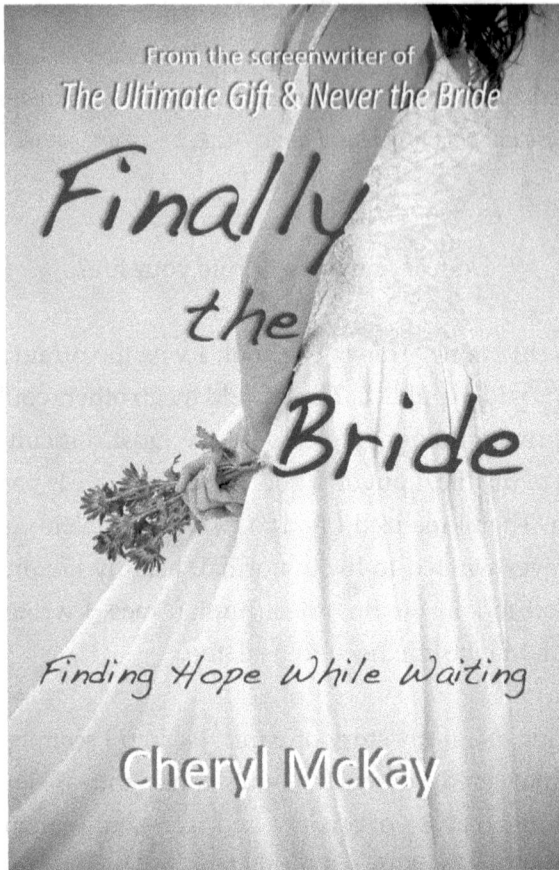

From the screenwriter of
The Ultimate Gift & Never the Bride

Finally the Bride

Finding Hope While Waiting

Cheryl McKay

From the Back Cover of *Finally the Bride: Finding Hope While Waiting*:

Why Would God Care About My Love Life?

From the woman behind the screenplay and novel, *Never the Bride*, comes a roller coaster of a love story with God. Cheryl McKay pulls no punches about what it's really like to be single, with your age creeping up, and no end in sight to the wait for love and marriage. It seems that many years ago, God asked Cheryl to surrender the pen she was using to write her love story. All He wanted was carte blanche. No problem, right?

Cheryl tentatively conceded—that is, until it became apparent that the Almighty had no intention of conforming to her writing schedule, much less the tick of her biological clock. In fact, He blew every deadline she ever attempted to set. As romance seemed to pass Cheryl by, she couldn't help but question: Could God really be trusted to bring her the love of her life?

Written during a long wait, this book opens up Cheryl's painfully honest, personal journals. She explores what it's like to enlist in God's Marriage Boot Camp, and how to survive singlehood year after solitary year. She wrestles with her Creator over multiple best friends that never see her "that way." Then there are those lists of what she wanted—you know, the ones she revised a billion times then laminated for safekeeping. She watches, bewildered, as much younger women find love that seems to elude her.

Through it all, she falls head over heels for a God who proves Himself to be as resistant to her controls as He is faithful beyond her wildest dreams. Are you still waiting? Have you lost hope? Venture to victory with a woman who knows just how hard it is to wait for the day when you are *Finally the Bride*.

This book includes a collection of real-life, God-written love stories by such authors as SQuire Rushnell & Louise DuArt (*God Winks Series, Couples Who Pray*), and Victorya Michaels Rogers (*Finding a Man Worth Keeping*).

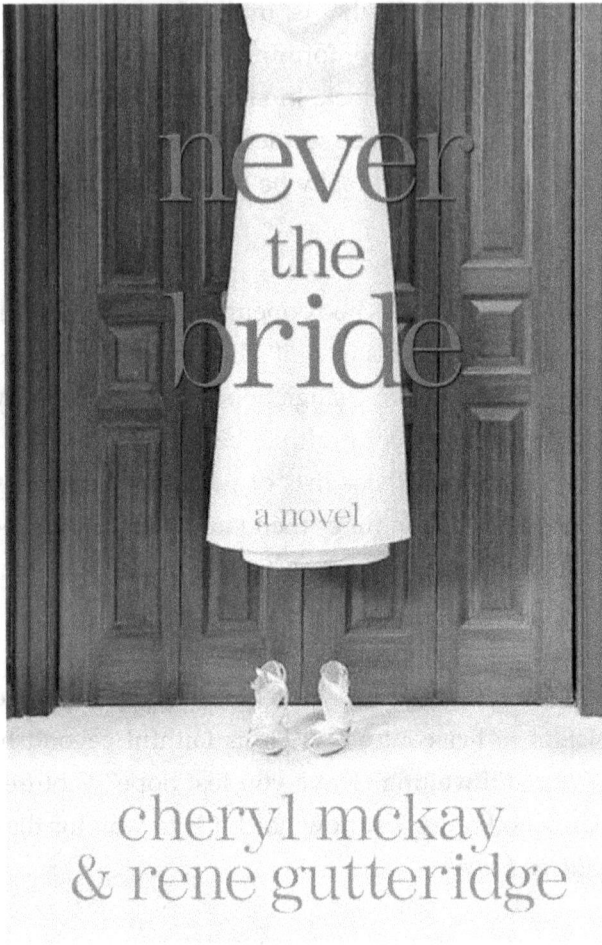

NEVER THE BRIDE a novel by Cheryl McKay & Rene Gutteridge
Published by Waterbrook Press

www.ingramcontent.com/pod-product-compliance
Lightning Source LLC
Chambersburg PA
CBHW050129280326
41933CB00010B/1311